DIANO ACCOMPANIMENT

CELTIC FOLKSONGS

FOR ALL AGES

JAMES CURNOW
TIMOTHY CAMPBELL

Order Number: CMP 1036-05-401

James Curnow, Timothy Campbell
Celtic Folksongs for all ages
Piano Accompaniment

CD Accompaniment tracks created by James L. Hosay

CD number: 19-063-3 CMP
ISBN 90-431-2296-3

CELTIC FOLK SONGS FOR ALL AGES

INTRODUCTION

This book is a sampling of rich tunes and ballads specifically distinctive to the cultures of Scotland, Newfoundland and Ireland. Initially associated with everyday rural activities, these memorable melodies have been married with colorful accompaniments to offer a variety of musical settings for all performers.

The accompaniment CD (included in the solo book) provides all musicians the opportunity to perform for organized gatherings or spontaneous productions among friends and relatives. There are two tracks for each tune. The first track includes a sample performance of the solo with the accompaniment. The second track is just the accompaniment, allowing the soloist to play along. So, delight in the richness of *"CELTIC FOLK SONGS FOR ALL AGES"* and continue the spirit with which folk music has been passed down through cultures near and far.

INSTRUMENTATION GUIDE

C Instrument (CMP 1031-05)	-	Piccolo, Flute, Oboe, or any Mallet Percussion instrument.
Bb Instrument (CMP 1032-05)	-	Bb Clarinet, Bb Bass Clarinet, Bb Cornet, Bb Trumpet, Bb Flugel Horn, Bb Tenor Saxophone, Bb Trombone T.C., Bb Euphonium/Baritone T.C., Bb Tuba T.C.
Eb Instrument (CMP 1033-05)	-	Eb Alto Clarinet, Eb Alto Saxophone, Eb Baritone Saxophone, Eb Tuba T.C.
F/Eb Instrument (CMP 1034-05)	-	F/Eb Horn
Bass Clef Instrument (CMP 1035-05)	-	Cello, Double Bass, Bassoon, Trombone B.C., Euphonium/Baritone B.C., Tuba B.C.
Piano Accompaniment (CMP 1036-05)		

JAMES CURNOW

James Curnow was born in Port Huron, Michigan and raised in Royal Oak, Michigan. He lives in Nicholasville, Kentucky where he is president, composer, and educational consultant for Curnow Music Press, Inc. of Wilmore, Kentucky, publishers of significant music for concert band and brass band. He also serves as Composer-in-residence (Emeritus) on the faculty of Asbury College in Wilmore, Kentucky, and is editor of all music publications for The Salvation Army in Atlanta, Georgia.

His formal training was received at Wayne State University (Detroit, Michigan) and at Michigan State University (East Lansing, Michigan), where he was a euphonium student of Leonard Falcone, and a conducting student of Dr. Harry Begian. His studies in composition and arranging were with F. Maxwell Wood, James Gibb, Jere Hutchinson, and Irwin Fischer.

James Curnow has taught in all areas of instrumental music, both in the public schools (five years), and on the college and university level (twenty-six years). He is a member of several professional organizations, including the American Bandmasters Association, College Band Directors National Association and Wind Ensembles and the American Society of Composers, Authors and Publishers (ASCAP). In 1980 he received the National Band Association's Citation of Excellence. In 1985, while a tenured Associate Professor at the University of Illinois, Champaign-Urbana, Mr. Curnow was honored as an outstanding faculty member. Among his most recent honors are inclusion in Who's Who in America, Who's Who in the South and Southwest, and Composer of the Year (1997) by the Kentucky Music Teachers Association and the National Music Teachers Association. He has received annual ASCAP standard awards since 1979.

As a conductor, composer and clinician, Curnow has traveled throughout the United States, Canada, Australia, Japan and Europe where his music has received wide acclaim. He has won several awards for band compositions including the ASBDA/Volkwein Composition Award in 1977 (*Symphonic Triptych*) and 1979 (*Collage for Band*), the ABA/Ostwald Award in 1980 (*Mutanza*) and 1984 (Symphonic Variants for Euphonium and Band), the 1985 Sixth International Competition of Original Compositions for Band (*Australian Variants Suite*), and the 1994 Coup de Vents Composition Competition of Le Havre, France (*Lochinvar*).

Curnow has been commissioned to write over two hundred works for concert band, brass band, orchestra, choir and various vocal and instrumental ensembles. His published works now number well over four hundred. His most recent commissions include the Tokyo Symphony Orchestra (*Symphonic Variants for Euphonium and Orchestra*), the United States Army Band (Pershing's Own, Washington, D.C.-Lochinvar, Symphonic Poem for Winds and Percussion), Roger Behrend and the DEG Music Products, Inc. and Willson Band Instrument Companies (*Concerto for Euphonium and Orchestra*), the Olympic Fanfare and Theme for the Olympic Flag (Atlanta Committee for the Olympic Games, 1996), the Kentucky Music Teachers Association/National Music Teachers Association in 1997 (*On Poems of John Keats for String Quartet*) and Michigan State University Bands (John Whitwell, Director of Bands) in honor of David Catron's twenty-six years of service to the university and the university bands (*Ode And Epinicion*).

TIMOTHY CAMPBELL

Timothy Campbell was born in Guelph, Ontario, Canada. He currently lives in Manchester, Connecticut where he teaches K – 12 instrumental and choral music for Cornerstone Christian School. He is also the personnel manager and contractor for the Summer Music Festival orchestra in New London, Connecticut, where he has worked with such artists as Jane Glover, Robert Levin, Larry Rachleff, Norman Krieger, Donald Pippen, and Johnny Mathis.

He received his undergraduate degree from Asbury College in theory and composition. While attending Asbury he studied with James Curnow and garnered such accolades as the Kentucky Music Educators Composition Award and the Penniston Honors Competition awards for piano and composition. Under a full scholarship, he went on to the University of Connecticut where he completed his master's degree in music theory.

TABLE OF CONTENTS

AIKEN DRUM

Scottish Folk Song
Arr. Timothy Campbell (ASCAP)

AIKEN DRUM 2

AIKEN DRUM 3

BELIEVE ME, IF ALL THOSE
ENDEARING YOUNG CHARMS

Irish Folk Song
Arr. Timothy Campbell (ASCAP)

BELIEVE ME, IF ALL THOSE ENDEARING YOUNG CHARMS 2

JACK WAS EVERY INCH A SAILOR

Newfoundland Folk Song
Arr. James Curnow (ASCAP)

JACK WAS EVERY INCH A SAILOR 2

JACK WAS EVERY INCH A SAILOR 3

THE ASH GROVE

Welsh Folk Song
Arr. Timothy Campbell (ASCAP)

THE ASH GROVE 2

I'LL TELL ME MA

Irish Folk Song
Arr. Timothy Campbell (ASCAP)

THE BLUEBELLS OF SCOTLAND

Scottish Folk Song
Arr. James Curnow (ASCAP)

THE BLUEBELLS OF SCOTLAND 3

I'S THE B'Y

Newfoundland Folk Song
Arr. Timothy Campbell (ASCAP)

LOCH LOMOND

Scottish Folk Song
Arr. Timothy Campbell (ASCAP)

LOCH LOMOND 2

LOCH LOMOND 3

TOO-RA-LOO-RA-LOO-RAL

(That's An Irish Lullaby)

Irish Folk Song
Arr. Timothy Campbell (ASCAP)

TOO-RA-LOO-RA-LOO-RAL 2

LUKEY'S BOAT

Newfoundland Folk Song
Arr. Timothy Campbell (ASCAP)

LUKEY'S BOAT 2

WHEN IRISH EYES ARE SMILING

Irish Folk Song
Arr. Timothy Campbell (ASCAP)

WHEN IRISH EYES ARE SMILING 2

36

WHEN IRISH EYES ARE SMILING 3

MRS. MURPHY'S CHOWDER

Irish Folk Song
Arr. Timothy Campbell (ASCAP)

MRS. MURPHY'S CHOWDER 2

MOUNTAINS OF MOURNE

Irish Folk Song
Arr. Timothy Campbell (ASCAP)

Copyright © 2005 by Curnow Music Press, Inc.

MOUNTAINS OF MOURNE 2

THE IRISH WASHERWOMAN

Irish Folk Song
Arr. Timothy Campbell (ASCAP)

THE IRISH WASHERWOMAN 2

THE IRISH WASHERWOMAN 3

MOLLY MALONE

Newfoundland Folk Song
Arr. Timothy Campbell (ASCAP)

MOLLY MALONE 2

MOLLY MALONE 3

WE'LL RANT AND WE'LL ROAR

Newfoundland Folk Song
Arr. Timothy Campbell (ASCAP)

WE'LL RANT AND WE'LL ROAR 2

WE'LL RANT AND WE'LL ROAR 3